SMYTHE LIBRARY

**Stamp this label with the date for return.
Contact the Librarian if you wish to renew this book.**

Methuen Drama

First published in Great Britain in 2001
Methuen Publishing Ltd

ISBN 0 413 76740 X

A CIP catalogue record for this book is available at the British Library

Typeset by Deltatype Ltd, Birkenhead, Merseyside
Transferred to digital printing 2004

Eden

by Eugene O'Brien

Methuen Drama

The Arts Council
An Chomhairle Ealaíon

The National Theatre gratefully acknowledges the financial
support from the Arts Council/An Chomhairle Ealaíon.

Eden
by Eugene O'Brien

Eden by Eugene O'Brien was first performed at the Peacock Theatre, Dublin on 18 January 2001. Press night was 24 January 2001.

The play is set in the present.

There will be one interval of 15 minutes

Billy	Don Wycherley
Breda	Catherine Walsh

Director	Conor McPherson
Designer	Bláithín Sheerin
Lighting Designer	Paul Keogan
Sound	Cormac Carroll
Stage Director	John Stapleton
Assistant Stage Manager	Gabby McGrath
Voice Coach	Andrea Ainsworth
Set	Abbey Theatre Workshop
Costumes	Abbey Theatre Wardrobe Department

Please note that the text of the play which appears in this volume may be changed during the rehearsal process and appear in a slightly altered form in performance.

Eugene O'Brien Author

As an actor, Eugene has worked with Storytellers, Corn Exchange, Bickerstaffe, Calypso, Barnstorm, Loose Canon and Glasshouse theatre companies. He appeared in the Abbey Theatre production of **Tarry Flynn** which toured to the Royal National Theatre, London. His film and television work includes **Trojan Eddie, Durango, A Secret Affair, Soap, Life in the Fast Lane, The Birthday, Bite to Eat, Ballykissangel,** DDU and **Fair City**. He has written two monologues, **America 87** and **Checking for Squirrels,** both produced by Black Box Theatre Company. He co-wrote the short films **Cold Turkey** and **America - A Movie**, as well as **The Nest,** a radio play for RTE.

Conor McPherson Director

Born in Dublin in 1971, Conor attended UCD where he began to write and direct. He graduated with an MA in Philosophy in 1993 and co-founded Fly by Night Theatre Company to produce new plays. These included **Rum & Vodka** and **The Good Thief** which won him the Stewart Parker Award. He became writer-in-residence at the Bush Theatre, London where he directed **This Lime Tree Bower** (Meyer-Whitworth Award, Guinness/Royal National Theatre Award, Thames TV Award) and **St Nicholas** which transferred to New York winning Brian Cox the Lucille Lortell Award for Best Actor. **The Weir** was written for the Royal Court in 1997. It transferred to the West End and ran for over two and a half years, winning numerous awards including the Laurence Olivier Award for Best Play, the Critics' Circle Award, the Evening Standard Award and the George Devine Award. It then played in Dublin at the Gate Theatre before transferring to Broadway where it ran for nine months. **Dublin Carol** opened the newly rebuilt Royal Court in February 2000. It was also seen at the 2000 Dublin Theatre Festival where it was nominated for Best Irish Production. Conor's film work includes the screenplay for **I Went Down** for which he won the IFTA Award for Best Screenplay and the Best Screenplay Award and Jury Prize at San Sebastian. He wrote and directed **Saltwater** which has also received numerous awards including the IFTA Award for Best Screenplay and the CICAE Awards for Best Film at the 2000 Berlin Film Festival. He directed **Endgame** as part of *Beckett on Film* starring Michael Gambon and David Thewlis. His new play **Port Authority** opens in London in February 2001, transferring to Dublin's Gate Theatre in April.

Bláithín Sheerin Designer

Bláithín trained in sculpture and performance art at NCAD and in theatre design at Motley @ Riverside Studios, London. Previous work at the Abbey and Peacock Theatres includes **As the Beast Sleeps** and **You Can't Take it with You**. She was Design Consultant on **Alices's Adventures in Wonderland/Alice Through the Looking Glass**, Blue Raincoat/Peacock Partners. Other designs include **The Comedy of Errors**, RSC, **Our Father**, Almeida Theatre, **The Importance of Being Earnest**, West Yorkshire Playhouse, **Juno and the Paycock**, Lyric Theatre, **The Beckett Festival** (composite set design), Gate Theatre, John Jay Theatre, New York. She has also designed for Druid, Groundwork, Charabanc, Red Kettle, TEAM, Second Age, Fishamble, Galloglass and Prime Cut. Her designs for Rough Magic include **The Whisperers, The School for Scandal, Northern Star, Pentecost, The Way of the World, The Dogs, Digging for Fire** and **Love and a Bottle**. **Pentecost** was performed at The Kennedy Center, Washington as part of the Island: Arts from Ireland Festival, May 2000. Most recently she designed **The Fourth Wise Man** at the Ark.

Paul Keogan Lighting Designer

Born in Dublin, Paul studied drama at the Samuel Beckett Centre, Trinity College Dublin and Glasgow University. Previous work at the Abbey and Peacock Theatres includes **Melonfarmer, The Electrocution of Children, Amazing Grace, The Passion of Jerome, Living Quarters, Making History, The Map Maker's Sorrow, Cúirt an Mheán Oíche, The Tempest, Treehouses, Mrs. Warren's Profession, Down the Line** and **Tartuffe**. Paul worked as a freelance lighting designer, mostly with dance companies, before joining the Project Arts Centre as Production Manager from 1994 until 1996. His designs include **Down Onto Blue, Danti Dan** and **Mrs Sweeney** for Rough Magic, **The Silver Tassie** at the Almeida Theatre, **The Gay Detective** at Project Arts Centre, **Electroshock** and **Quartet** for Bedrock Productions, **The Duchess of Malfi, The Spanish Tragedy, The White Devil** and **Hamlet** for Loose Canon Theatre Company, **The Whiteheaded Boy** for Barabbas, **Much Ado About Nothing** for Bickerstaffe at Kilkenny Castle. His opera designs include **La Boheme, L'Elisir d'Amore** and **The Marriage of Figaro** for Opera Ireland, **That Dublin Mood, The Lighthouse** and **The Rake's Progress** for Opera Theatre Company. Dance designs include **Ballads,**

Seasons and **Straight with Curves** for CoisCéim Dance Theatre, **Sweat** and **Beautiful Tomorrow** for Mandance, **Three Piece Suite** and **Chimera** for Daghdha Dance Company, **SAMO** for Blok & Steel. Recent designs include **Angel-Babel** for Operating Theatre, **Quay West** for Bedrock Productions, **The Wishing Well**, an outdoor projection project in Kilkenny, **Without Hope or Fear** for Mandance, **The Makropulos Case** for Opera Zuid in the Netherlands, **Intimate Gold** for Irish Modern Dance Theatre and **Lady Macbeth of Mtsensk** and **Madame Butterfly** for Opera Ireland.

Catherine Walsh Breda

Catherine trained at the Samuel Beckett Centre, Trinity College. Performances at the Abbey and Peacock Theatres include **Translations, Kevin's Bed, Love in the Title** which toured Ireland, San Jose and Singapore and **At Swim-Two-Birds**. Other theatre work includes **Phaedra, A Christmas Carol**, Gate Theatre, **Buddleia**, Passion Machine, **Werewolves**, Druid Theatre Company, **Licking the Marmalade Spoon**, Baois Productions at Project Arts Centre, **From Both Hips**, Fishamble Theatre Company, **The House of Bernarda Alba**, Charabanc Theatre Company, **The Chastitute**, Gaiety Theatre, **Big Maggie**, Cork Opera House, **Skychair** with Alice Maher and Trevor Knight at project @ the mint and **Home** by Paul Mercier, Wheatfield Prison. Film and television work includes **Family, The Ambassador** (BBC) **Before I Sleep** (RTE) and **The Last September**.

Don Wycherley Billy

Don began his acting career at the Abbey Theatre in 1992 and since then he has played numerous roles in many productions including **Away Alone, The Honey Spike, The Last Apache Reunion, The Winter Thief, Famine, Tarry Flynn, Portia Coughlan, The Muesli Belt, The House** and **Translations**. Television credits include Fr Aidan in **Ballykissangel**, Eugene in **Black Day at Blackrock**, Fr Cyril Macduff in **Father Ted** and Seán in **Filleann an Feall** for TG4, which he also wrote. Film credits include **The Last of the High Kings, Michael Collins, I Went Down, Widows Peak, The General, One Man's Hero** and **When Brendan met Trudy**.

Amharclann Na Mainistreach
The National Theatre Society Limited

Amharclann Na Mainistreach
The National Theatre Society Limited

The Arts Council
An Chomhairle Ealaíon

Eden

Billy I'll tell ye one thing and I won't tell ye two things, she is fucking gorgeous. (*He sighs*) . . . Standing in the golf links bar on captain's night: jazz, prizes and fuckin' speeches and now drink, and lookin' at her: Ernie and Evonne Egan's daughter – Imelda.

I'm talkin' to her da at the bar but I'm lookin' at her – Jeasus. Now her ma is getting up to leave and I know full well the two Boylans, the middle ones, the bucks, are sensin', knowin' that it's time. Ernie's with me at the bar talkin' shorthand, Evonne's outside with the Boylans and the inside of their Hiace will witness the sights and sounds of a fifty-five-year-old mother of four, and a pair a twenty-somethin's ridin' like the clappers.

Poor fuckin' Ernie talks ol' shorthand to me, not a clue, the fuckin' gomie, and I wonder how such a beautiful ride of a thing, their young one Imelda, who is now inside jivin' to the jazz, could ever have been a product of his sack. 'I had a twenty-five footer to the back nine eleventh,' says Ernie. 'Really, Ernie, did ye hole it?' I say. 'No,' says Ernie. 'Just a fraction past.' 'Ye didn't hole it, Ernie, Jeasus, ye'd hole nothin', ye wouldn't score in a brothel with a ten-pound note stuck to your lad,' I say and he laughs. 'Ah yeah, that's me, wouldn't hit flyin' elephants,' and I laugh and take a big swalla of the red diesel and think sure isn't it nearly as much crack here, talkin' shite to Ernie and imaginin' what his wife and the boys are doin' in the van as actually bein' out there with them.

Anyways it's not Evonne that I'm after, oh no, it's her young one, Imelda . . . Jeasus, Tony tried her one night, nothin' on, and Tony's rode the range. He is James Galway, the man with the golden flute . . . He's the reason I'm here, in the fuckin' golf club, never hit a ball in me life, wouldn't drive nails but Tony's played for years: he's James Galway and I'm not, I'm strapped, saddled, married . . .

Anyway she's back – the daughter, not the ma – she's still outside, in the van. Ernie is talkin' to Sergeant Ryan now, who's Mickey Monk drunk and talkin' shorthand about the time Fergus Farrell's head was found in the bog, and I'm wonderin' how I could get talkin' to Imelda . . .

Last Saturday, this night last week, drink after Spiders night-club in Feggy Fennelly's house and I'm fairly Mickey Monk and I'm talkin' fierce shorthand, load of me hole rigmarole, ye know, and she's listenin' with the crowd and laughin' and I was on, I was flyin', and now it's here again, the holy trinity . . . Friday, the beezneez, Johnstownbridge, Saturday, here in the fuckin' golf links but usually Spiders, Sunday, Mac's, late bar, and she'll be there too, set it up tonight and then tomorrow night . . . I will be James Galway. My flute will be pure gold and they'll all know, in Brophy's, Bob's bar, Flanagan's, the Top It Up, the Corner House, Kavanagh's, they'll all know, in every bar in the town that I rode Imelda Egan and Tony didn't.

I take a swalla and see that Evonne's swanned back in – not a bother on her – and the two Boylans not far behind her, with their mickeys still wet and now they're chattin' to Ernie who's offerin' to buy them drink. Evonne passes by and I say, 'Havin' a good night.' 'Ah yeah,' she says, and I congratulate her on the best gross or net or whatever bit of useless fuckin' crystal she's won and I buy her a gin and tonic as an excuse to get sittin' with Imelda.

I remember from the night in Feggy's that Imelda was goin' for some office job in Jimmy McGoldrick's bodybuilders, so we're chattin' about that and I can't help looking at her and thinking how I'd come like a cat outta a skylight if she even looked at it, and this puts me off and I hesitate like a fuckin' gnoc, which lets her friend get in with somethin' about Jennifer Cullen comin' home from Australia.

I've no fuckin' drink left but I don't want to lose me seat beside Imelda and where the fuck is the man I came out here with? Tony, James Galway and now Ernie has arrived over with some young fella, not from the town, and they're talkin' about some puttin' green thing, some portable ten-

foot-long yoke that folds up so ye can practise in your house
and I don't know the fuck why I'm listenin' to this. But
anyways – the young fella sells these things round the
country and he's tellin' us about his mad uncle Gilbert who
invented the greens. He was talkin' to Seve Ballesteros at the
Irish Open sayin' how Seve could take one home to Spain,
for free, he could put one in the back of his car this instant,
but Seve declined and I'm eyein' the bar and Lee Trevino
wasn't impressed either so the uncle went out to RTE and
set the puttin' green up on the main stairs sayin' that he
wouldn't move it until Gay Byrne himself came down to
have a go and put him on the *Late Late*. So Byrne came
down and agreed to have it on as long as Uncle Gilbert was
nowhere near the studio. We're all laughin', 'cause he told it
well like, an' now Evonne wants one for the house and Ernie
sayin' that they're great yokes and it's all a pain in the Nat
King Cole 'cause Imelda and the friend are leavin' to talk to
Geraldine Cullen, sister of Jennifer who's comin' back from
Australia.

So I head straight to the bar and get a pint and a short,
keepin' an eye out for Tony, takin' a gape into the dance
floor, slow set is on, and the Sergeant is mickey standin'
behind me, givin' me a nod, even though I'm from St John's
Park and I shouldn't really be here, but I am, so fuck him
and the shutters is comin' down so I order more drink –
when finally I spot Tony at the other end of the bar.

He's with Eilish Moore, who's back from England. She's a
great pal of the wife's, of Breda's, and she's separated from
some English cunt and I know Tony'll be trying to ride her
tonight and I don't feel the Mae West, I don't feel, wha' is it,
whether I'm comin' or goin' or somethin' and I don't like
this kinda crack, this mad as a March hare in spring crack,
fightin' it. I'm swallowin', atin' the glass. It's like last
Saturday night in Spiders , this same feelin' – which didn't
go until I was properly mickey in Feggy's house and talkin'
shite.

I hear Eilish laughin', look to see Tony takin' a drag of his

smoke, real close together and I'm ragin' 'cause we won't be
able to stay up in his house drinkin' now 'cause he'll want to
be at her and I can't see Imelda anywhere, only her da and
ma, Ernie and Evonne leavin', glasses been collected and
Knobby Cummins shoutin', 'COME ON, LADS, WILL
YES GO HOME FOR FUCK'S SAKE.' So I take a walk
into the bar 'cause I hear girls laughin' but it's only the fat
Corcoran ones on their way out.

Tony shouts at me to come on, he'll take me into the town,
he's in great form and Eilish shites on about Breda in the
front seat all the way home and says that she'll be round to
see her tomorrow and they leave me outside the door as
Tony speeds the pair of them up the town . . .

I'm lyin' beside her now, listenin' to her breathin' and I'm
more mickey than I thought I was 'cause I'm thinkin' of all
sorts . . . *The little fella that I pulled outta the sea that time when I
was only young meself, how he lay there on the sand with not a twitch
outta him, us kids starin' down and a mother grabbin' him up roarin'
and harin' on up the beach* . . . and I wonder did he ever live?
It's somethin' comes into me head the odd time and I think
of my two girls safely asleep next door.

Breda shifts slightly in the bed – she's definitely lost the
weight – and I hear the guard dogs barkin' up beyond in the
granary and I wish I was in Tony's sittin' room drinkin'
whiskey and talkin' shite about Imelda Egan and how I was
goin' to get off with her.

Breda   I'm watchin' this woman and she's in tears . . .
because her daughter was murdered by your one Myra
Hindley, and there's talk about lettin' her out. 'Over my
dead body,' the woman is sayin' on *Kenny Live.*

It's fierce depressin' to see someone so angry and upset,
which makes me turn me eyes from the tele to the clock,
and think about the book upstairs, as it'd usually be time for
the book. I keep it in one of the suitcases, safe enough in
there as Billy hasn't picked up a suitcase in years . . . Lord
Jahzzz . . . There's a fierce urge on me to tear upstairs, open

the case, root out the book and ever so carefully open page
174, fierce slowly, page 174 . . .

To the harem where the woman is chosen from a whole rake of women,
picked out by these guards and they escort her to the sultan's tent, and
her husband, who had never satisfied her, is there, forced to look on,
while the guards go to work on her, both of them like, at the same time,
rale slow, getting' her ready for the big sultan, and she's eventually
brought before him and starts to, ye know, suck him off which she's rale
into, describin' his cock and all this and the husband can't bear lookin'
at this any longer, breaks free of the guards, takes her from behind and
they all come together in one huge amazin' orgasm and . . . and . . .
no, I won't, not tonight, 'cause I'm savin' meself, I'll leave
the book where it is.

It was me best friend Eilish gave me the book, about a year
ago, before she went off to England with Cliff, he was this
English fella from London that she'd met up in Dublin while
she was nursin', he was named after Cliff Richard, good-
lookin' fella, cockney fella, rale *EastEnders*, and they'd come
down to visit and me and Eilish were still rale close, so we'd
talk, oh Jesus, we liked to talk, and I knew that he didn't
like that. But anyways she was mad about him and moved
lock and stock to London, about a year ago as I said, and
she left me this book 'cause she had no need for it any more
as herself and Cliff were like animals, she said, the details
ye'd get, in bed, on the stairs, in the kitchen, goin' down on
each other in the back of a taxi in London one time and
bein' thrown out and all this and she'd be tellin' me all this.

Well I couldn't keep it in any longer, I was burstin'. I let it
all out, about me and Billy 'cause it's both of our faults, not
just him. I made her swear to keep it to herself and she
swore that she would and she suggests counsellin' but sure
Billy would never in a million years go near a counsellor, no
way José, so she says well, in the meantime, while yes get
sorted out, there's this book I'll give ye, 'cause a woman is a
woman, she laughed and the next day, the day before she
leaves for England, she brings it round to the house.

It's this yoke written by an American one who got all these women writin' in to her, describin' their sexual fantasies, a collection of them like, rale mad ones some of them, bondage and rape and Alsatians, all that crack, which like I wasn't gone on but there was quite a few that I did kinda go for, started to really get into, especally the one set in the harem so I gradually started to . . . you know . . . which I'd never really done before, I'd always stopped meself, a bit ashamed or embarrassed, whatever, so anyways of a Saturday evenin' he'd be gone out, and I wouldn't 'cause of me weight, so he'd be doin' his thing, and I . . . I'd be doin' my thing, when the two girls were in bed, with *Kenny Live* on behind me with the sound turned up.

But tonight I'm not, I pour a vodka instead, he's out in the golf links tonight with Tony Tyrell, his friend, James Galway, as they do call him, 'cause of all the women he's had, the man with the golden flute, and I know that Billy thinks that he's great, envies him a bit, ye know, and I'm sure that he does be lookin' at young ones himself . . .

Eilish is out there too, she's back this two weeks, she left Cliff, 'cause he was gettin' fierce possessive, rale thick with her over even half chattin' to a fella, nearly hittin' her after a nightclub 'cause he thought she'd been chattin' too much to one of his mates, he raised his arm and that was it, history, she bolted the next morning, it's great to have her back.

Eilish is goin' to be a great help to me tomorrow night. It's me big entrance into the pubs of the town, I'm goin' out for the first time in ages, 'cause I've lost the weight. She's callin' over and we'll end up in Mac's, and he will come home with me, I think he will, 'cause I've made the effort, I've lost the weight. I met this one at the women's group, she's from Knob Hill, married to the manager of the shoe factory, fierce nice woman but. Got me on to this special diet-plan thing and it's worked, and I know that he's noticed, we've been getting on a bit better. Like he even . . . Last Saturday night when he got into bed beside me, it'd always be late and he'd always be locked . . . but last Saturday he put his arm around me. I moved closer into him, he kissed the back of me, I turned me face around to him, and then he kissed me again and I thought just for a second that he was goin' to, ye know, but he drifted off . . . his arm stayin' around me for a while . . . so do ye see what I'm sayin'? I think we can, you know, after Mac's tomorrow night, be a proper married couple again.

I'm up in the bed now, the head is racin', can't settle, *that fuckin' weighin' scales, me da, the family, in the kitchen, dreadin' me eyes for lookin' at him, lose some fuckin' weight, ye fat little fucker, it was his way, tryin' to do me good, shoutin' at me like he would at the under sixteen hurlin' team he trained, me sister cryin', me willin' the scales to change, to please him.*

Half asleep now, in betweeny nightmarey kinda thing, *the name, they had a name for me, they'd look around, they'd laugh and whisper . . . Sports day, long jump, sweaty and nervous as the crowd gathers around, my go after the next girl, confused as to where you jump from, you run and then jump from . . . where? The board? After the board? Wipin' me brow, the volume risin', chantin' my name, 'BREDA . . . BREDA', louder and louder until I have to take off, move as fast as I can, run, run, run, right through, straight through, forget to jump, and now they're all havin' a field day at their field day, laughin' like hyenas, chantin' that name, that other name then whisperin' and sniggerin', in the hall, school disco, walls outside the chipper, nights at the pictures, that name. Eilish always there with boys chattin' to her, all types, the sporty, the brainy, the shy ones, the ugly ones, the cute ones, all there chattin' to her, sniggerin' the name at me, the name . . .*

He's home, heavy cigarette breathin', shoes against floor, my eyes open now, it's Billy home but I don't let on to be awake, in beside me now, his breathin' right in beside me. But no arm comes around me this week and there's no kiss. That's all right, though, because I'll drift off again, try to think of tomorrow night, look forward to tomorrow night when things will be different . . . I hear the dogs barkin' above in the granary and I think of the book and for a moment I wish that I was back in the harem, being chosen, out of all the women, being escorted by the guards, to the sultan, who's waitin' for me above in his tent.

Billy   I'll tell ye one thing and I won't tell ye two things, I open me eyes, it's about eleven, and I feel fairly rotten, not fully poisoned but near enough. There's this paintin' in the room, directly opposite me when I wake up, some yoke one of Breda's crowd gave us for the wedding and there's these men in a field near a stream workin' with hay, and it's sunny and I used t'hate the fuckin' thing but now I don't mind it and I'm kinda starin' at it, in a kinda hung-over googly-eyed way and I'm imaginin' that I'm in it, in the paintin', on some big estate and Imelda Egan is a parlourmaid or somethin' and we get it together behind this big tree and I'm as fuckin' hard and she's lovin' it.

And Breda comes in, not into the paintin', into the bedroom, and says nothin' and she goes out again. I don't feel much like atin' anythin' but I have some Frosties and the two girls are fuckin' roarin' and I tell them they'll get no sweets from O'Connor's if they don't sha' up and they kinda sha' up and Breda's askin' me about last night in the golf links and I get into worse humour 'cause I remember she wants to come to Mac's tonight so I just grunt, bein' rale impotent, buried in the paper, readin' about yesterday's soccer 'cause the boys will be shitin' on about it in the pub and ye kinda have to know what went on.

Walkin' down the road now, I meet Feggy and him and meself, two of the Banana O'Briens and the Skunk, who thank Jeasus has had a wash as it's a Sunday, stand at the back of the church until the Mass is over and I remember nothin' about it except your man who was up the tree, Zacchaeus, and I start callin' Feggy Zacchaeus, just to brown him, until we get to the Corner House for the two before the dinner.

And by Jeasus, who's sittin' up at the bar only Brefine Grehan, back from London, the boys heard he was in

trouble again for somethin', so he's home and he's bein'
fierce friendly. 'How's the boys?' 'Not a bother, Brefine,' we
say back and I kinda wanta talk more to him 'cause we
always kinda got on in school and that, fuckin' gas, a mad
cunt but, tried to break into it, one summer, the school,
durin' the holidays, the two of us, for the crack but I fell off
a wall and the squad was called, fuckin' creeled meself and
Brefine lookin' down at me breakin' his shite. Now anyways
I want to stay with him at the bar only it's a bit awkward.
Ye see, he tried to get off with Big Banana's mot Therese
the year before and there was a fierce row, and here I am,
stuck between Little Banana and Middle Banana, so like it's
not on, but everyone's been rale civil and we go to sit down
but Brefine takes a big swalla and says that he'll see us in
Mac's later on . . .

We all know that Big Banana will be there too and there'll
probably be war but Little Banana and Middle Banana
aren't goin' to say anythin' just now 'cause they're scared of
their shite of him so instead they ask me about the golf links
and I ask about Spiders and I'm feelin' better now 'cause as
Tony does say the new beer is meetin' the old beer inside in
your system and they're getting' on fierce well.

Breda   May Moynihan is tellin' me about her eye
operation outside the church after the half-nine and about
every ailment in the town and the girls whingein' for to go
home but sure ye have to stop and listen to her. 'Lil Coinin's
lookin' very bad, the stroke really took it out of her.'

Eventually arrived home now to cartoons for them and Billy
lyin' in the bed with his hung-over stare, spaced out, in his
own world above in the room, I say nothin' and he's down
now without a word for the cat. I can't quite remember how
long it's been like this, things just seem to get set in a
pattern . . .

He heads off out and I do the joint and iron me dress for
tonight, the nerves startin' at me, quick check in the mirror,
reassure meself, bolster meself up, and then I join the girls

and laugh at the big bear dressed up as a monkey singin' 'I
wanna be like you'.

I watch this with them until I hear the bang of the back
door announcin' that he's back, and whatever happened
him at Mass or the pub he's arrived back in great form, full
of chat, jokin' with the girls and I love that because that's
the way it should be all the time.

He takes them out for sweets, and they're gone longer than
usual, which is great 'cause they'll be tired and go to bed
with no fuss, and he helps me with their tea before he leaves.
Beside him in the kitchen I thought of his arm around me in
the bed the week before and for the first time in, oh Jeasus,
don't ask me, I felt that he wouldn't mind if I leaned across
and chanced a quick kiss, just on his cheek, and he didn't
seem to mind and I said that I'd see him later above in
Mac's and he said grand and I want to say more, I want to
say tonight's the night, wait till ye see me tonight, you'll
want me tonight.

But I don't and he's gone and I start gettin' ready thinkin' of
him stridin' through the crowd, the dry ice, stridin' through
to me, to ask me, 'Breda,' he said, 'Breda, do ye want to get
up, ye know to dance,' and we got up and he held me tight
and time stopped. 'I know this much is true.' I do me eyes
and laugh at what an eegot I am still able to recall every
second of that night, nearly eleven years on now.

Billy   I'm up at the bar gettin' the second ones when
there's this gaggle of laughin' comin' in the door and Jeasus
. . . it's Imelda, she'd never be in here at this time, look at
her and she's with Geraldine Cullen and her sister Jennifer
who's just this mornin' come in from Australia, and we say
hello and next minute Imelda is up at the bar beside me
orderin' drink and I've never talked to her sober, so I'm
feelin' all self-conscious and she's askin' me all about last
night and who was that one Tony was with and all this and
I can see that she's a bit balubous, and I have to take me
eyes off her lips that are movin' 'cause I know they'll only

put me off and I ask why she'd left so early, and she says, 'Why, did ye miss me?' and I say, 'A course I did, but sure didn't I know that I'd see ye in Mac's tonight,' and she says, and she smiles, that was the best part, she says, 'You'd be right, I'll see ye there,' and I go back with the pints and I feel rale excited, ye know, she smiled, she smiled . . . at me.

I'm in great form, atin' me dinner at home now, bein' rale chatty to Breda, 'Jeasus, that's a great bit of meat, did ye get it in Walsh's or up in Gaynor's?' and all this and she tells me that Amanda the babysitter's comin' at eight and Eilish is callin' round for her and they'll go to Flanagan's and head up to Mac's then, and I say sure that's grand, and I tell her that I met Eilish last night and don't mention that she went home with Tony 'cause I know Breda will knock great crack outta talkin' shite to Eilish herself about him.

I'm standin' in the hallway puttin' the girls' coats on when I look in at her in the livin' room and I'm thinkin' that she's definitely lost the weight and not lookin' at all bad. I walk the two girls down to O'Connor's for to get them the sweets, then back along the canal bank and wash the chocolate off their faces when we get home and even help Breda with their tea . . .

She tries to kiss me in the kitchen 'cause I'm bein' so nice and all that and I let her, just the one, like, 'cause I'm thinkin' of Imelda Egan and how she smiled at me, and there will probably be a do after Mac's in Jennifer Cullen's tonight, 'cause she's back from Australia . . . that's where it's goin' to happen, me and Imelda Egan, in front of everyone, and I serve the two little ones their tea and go upstairs to change.

Breda   Amanda the babysitter has arrived and I'm tryin' to make chat with her, but sure I can think of nothin' to say only the ol' shite that used t'bore me when I was her age, stuff about school and teachers that are still there that used t'teach me, but she's makin' an effort. 'Ah yeah, sexy-eyes Holton is still up there, I had him last year for pass maths.'

But I can see that she'd rather be left alone to read her magazines and watch tele so I go into the kitchen.

Eilish is late but sure that's no surprise. 'You'd be late for your own funeral,' I used t'say to her and she'd say, 'And I'll definitely be late for me own weddin', leave the fucker sweatin',' and she'd laugh, but she's never had to do that, ah there's been plenty of fellas, she went steady with Kenny Kerrigan the last year in school and a bit after, they used t' call him Chicken Gorge on account he had big lips, and there was a nurse fella from Kerry who was mad about her, proposed and everythin', I liked him but he was too quiet for Eilish, too kinda sensible, and I heard about but never met a Paul, a Gavin, a Patrick, a Jim, a Greg, a Barry and a Charlie who she said was the best in bed until she met your man Cliff of course. Funny how I can remember all of their names and if ye asked her she probably wouldn't be able to . . .

I pour a vodka, I wish she'd hurry up, I check meself again in the mirror in the hall, I think I look all right, hope I haven't overdone it, but sure I know Eilish wouldn't let me go outside the door lookin' like a gnoc. She's always looked out for me, even as we got older and the boys started to call me the name, she never turned her back on me, like so many of the others.

It's nine o'clock and just as I'm thinkin' of ringin' Eilish 'cause she's late even for her, she comes burstin' in the back door. 'Give us a drink.' In great form and sure she's tellin' me all about Tony and why she was late, spent the whole day in his flat, all day and she's laughin', who would ever have thought, me and Tony Tyrell, but all she wants is a bit of crack, after the cliffhanger, as she does call the English fella now, 'cause the cliffhanger was hard work. He was pure mule. We used t'say that to describe anythin' from a night out, to a long queue, to shite beer, to a bad snog, but it always meant that the thing was desperate, or disappointin', it was just pure mule.

But tonight wouldn't be, 'cause I'm havin' such crack with Eilish in the kitchen, laughin' 'cause I feel like a teenager. It's half-nine now and Eilish picks up her bag, swings it up on to her shoulder and says, 'OK, girlfriend, let's live it large!' and I gulp back the end of me vodka and follow her out the back door.

Billy   Headin' up the road, it's early yet, so the town hall isn't surrounded by cars, and Dominic Sexton's minibus has just landed from Clara and the under twelves football team pile out, roarin' and shoutin', so they must have won their match and Dominic has a big thick head on him 'cause he's had to listen to them all the way home and I'd say the Peggy Dell of sweat and Moby Dick in the bus would be enough to poison a rat.

I head further up the town, on the last lap of the holy trinity and there's not a bother on me, rarin' to go, feelin' good, like, you can tell by the way I use my walk that I'm a woman's man no time to talk, and all that shite, and I intend to settle on a high stool in Kavanagh's, for the one before meetin' the boys in the Corner House, a quiet one, relax the head, ye can do that in Kavanagh's, and I push in the door and Majella says, 'How's Billy,' and reaches for a glass, and I always imagine what she'd look like without the wig, and I only really know the Mouse Mahar and the Badger Fennelly, Feggy's older brother, under the tele, who grunt at me 'cause they're glued to some quiz yoke with your one who rides your man who plays the piano on the *Late Late*.

Then I hear another 'How's Billy' from the far end of the counter, and there he is, sittin' up, large as life and twice as ugly . . . it's fuckin' Brefine Grehan, half of me dreadin' me eyes for seein' him on account of the Bananas and the other half of me glad that he's here, ye know, a bit of the out of the ordinary shorthand, no, not shorthand, ye never really got shorthand from the Breff. That's what we used t'call him in school, before he went a bit mad, unpredictable, like, and we stopped hangin' around him. He went off to Dublin for a

while and he's been in London since, bar the odd few visits
and as the fella says it'd be fierce impotent not to join him
and it'd be safe enough in here anyways so I do. He pays for
me pint which is the Mae West and we're chattin' away, so I
ask him what the johnnymagorry is, like, why is he home?
He doesn't say anythin' for a while, just rolls a cigarette rale
carefully, so I look back to see some gomie winnin' a holiday
on the screen above the Mouse and the Badger.

Brefine is lightin' his smoke now, speakin' to me in a low
voice, there'd been a bit of trouble on the site he was
workin' on, and I ask him what happened as ye would, like,
and he tells me that they were all English on the site bar him
and this young fella from this lake in the middle a nowhere
called Blacksod Bay and that was his name, like Brefine
asked him one day what his rale name was and he said that
he didn't know, that he'd always been called Blacksod.

Now some of the other lads were all right, like the lads from
up the north, Leeds or Newcastle, but that he didn't like the
most of them, it'd be Paddy this and Paddy that and did ye
plant any bombs lately and all this and not lendin' fifty p for
a Coke on pay day when they knew that they'd get it back
that evenin', small things like that but there was this bastard
foreman, rale cunt, and he was makin' life hell for the young
Mayo fella, would have him doin' the heaviest stupidest
work and gettin' at him all the time in front of the others.

So's anyways one night Brefine and the young Blacksod fella
are off their heads on drugs and Brefine decides that they'll
break into the site, but this wasn't like tryin' to break into
the school years ago, where I ended up with a sore hole and
Brefine had a good laugh at me. He wasn't laughin' this
time 'cause whatever happened didn't Blacksod end up
fallin' off the buildin' and Brefine was so far gone, on the
drugs, like, that he didn't wait around, he just bolted. This
was all last week and Brefine doesn't know whether the poor
young fella is alive or brown bread.

I say, 'Jeasus, that's rough, Brefine,' but it's all gettin' a bit

fuckin' heavy so I order more drink and go for a slash. Not
bein' able to stop meself thinkin' of the young fella that I
pulled outta the sea that time, and whether he's alive or
brown bread. Because sometimes I get a mad notion that he
is alive and that he's somebody famous and that the world
owes me some thanks for savin' him.

I spot the young fella who sells the puttin' greens comin' in,
I give him a big howareye. Time is marchin', it's time for
Mac's and we're startin' a pint so I may forget about the
boys in the Corner House and the young puttin' green fella
is introducin' himself, Eoghan is his name and he's tellin' us
that Ernie Egan had taken him for a drink after he'd sold
three greens and that it was grand until Ernie got a bit
mickey and started to as Eoghan put it 'bore the tits off
him'.

Now I don't want to walk into Mac's with Brefine on
account of the Bananas so I'm delighted that this Eoghan's
arrived 'cause maybe if he comes with us it wouldn't look as
bad or somethin' and as I'm thinkin' this Brefine starts
askin' about Breda and the ages of the two girls and I laugh.
'Ah sure ye'd be strangled with them,' thinkin' that a fella
like him would have no interest in all that load of me hole
rigmarole family crack, but he's sayin' that I'm lucky and all
this, that it's the best thing can happen a man, fierce odd,
like, comin' from him, soundin' like somebody's da. But
then I realise that I am somebody's da and I kinda laugh to
meself but I'm gettin' that queer feelin' again so I take a big
swalla but I'm thinkin' about Breda and how she's lost the
weight and how she'll be in Mac's tonight.

So I take another big swalla because I have to get back on
track, relax the head, and I think of Imelda Egan in the
painting, behind the big tree, me and her, me as hard as a
rock and her lovin' every minute of it . . . back on track,
time to skedaddle, so we drink up and I tell the young
puttin' green fella where we're goin' and he's delighted, says
somethin' about lonely B and Bs, delighted to be goin' on
somewhere, so we do. Mac's is fairly jammers, and I spot

Breda talkin' to Eilish and a few of the others, Feggy and the Skunk squashed in at the bar and there's no sign of the Bananas, thank the Lord lamb a Jeasus.

Breda I haven't seen the inside of Flanagan's pub this six or seven months, the warm blast of air hits me, the smoke, Quenchers Quinn behind the bar with his one hair still religiously combed across his bald skull, and young Derek Mangan who I used t'babysit beside him pullin' pints, I say me hellos and howareyes, heads turn ever so slightly to see me.

There's a knot in me stomach which gradually loosens as we sit at the bar with Sandra Scully and Therese Nolan, vodka is ordered and the two girls are fierce excited and announce that Therese is pregnant and we congratulate her and look down at the Big Banana O'Brien and all the O'Briens in the far corner, already fairly locked.

Me knotted stomach loosens more as the first of the vodkas goes down and we're all invited to a big party up in O'Briens' after the pub, but we say that we're headin' to Mac's and Sandra laughs. 'Jeez, ye'll pick up fuck all in there,' and suddenly she remembers the news about Tony and Eilish, so there's more screechin' and it's all girls together now and Jeasus I'm flyin' now and people are sayin' that I look well and I down another vodka and I have this warm, excited, whatd'yemacallit, and I suddenly realise what it is, I'm happy, I'm fuckin' happy, and let a laugh outta me, for no reason and the girls look at me and I try and shout for more drink off Quenchers Quinn and I'm goin' to savour every moment of this night.

Quenchers is tryin' to get rid of the Tex Donoghue, who's locked and won't go home. 'Take it to Missouri now, Tex,' he's sayin' to him and Tex roars back, 'Get the gun outta the wagon, John, we got some trouble in this here saloon,' and his friend John Dillon manages to steer him towards the door. 'Get the gun outta the wagon, John,' the Tex's still roarin'. Sandra starts on about the time the Tex was stopped by the guards in his Hiace which he had cut into a L-shaped pick-up and the guards had said to him that the van was in an illegal condition for a vehicle and the Tex was sayin', 'I didn't rightly know that, partner,' and he'd no tax or insurance. 'I didn't rightly know that, Officer,' and he'd got not one but four bald tyres. 'Excuse me, Officer,' said Tex. 'Better make that five, the one in the boot is the same,' and we all roar laughin', for ages, not even at the story, I just want to laugh.

Evonne Egan comes into the bar, I'd spotted the husband Ernie talkin' to some fella at the far end of the counter earlier on, the fella's just gone and Ernie is makin' a beeline for Evonne, who we don't really talk to, she'd be more golf links and all that, and they're behind us now and Ernie is fairly on, payin' her loads of attention, which she is clearly not into. 'Order us a drink there, Ernie.'

Ernie tries to get Quenchers Quinn's attention while babblin' on about the young fella he was with, somethin' about it must be a lonely ol' life, in a different town every night, sellin' his ol' greens, a lonely ol' life he says again and tries to squeeze her arm, which she avoids by reachin' for a fag and we're watchin' all this and Evonne knows that we are so she vamooses, skedaddles, with a little flick of her head back to Ernie, 'Bring it down here to me, when ye get served.'

I focus in on Ernie, I can't take me eyes off him, he seems to be lost for a moment, his half-smile, his eyes focused on somethin', behind the bar, the black and white dogs advertisin' the Scotch, somethin'. What's runnin' through his head? 'Cause I can hear Sandra and Therese mutterin' stories beside me about Evonne's latest activities, and I know that the boys from the golf links pull the piss outta him, 'cause I've heard Billy go on about it, 'cause Ernie's not a man, after half a bottle a gin, Evonne'll let anyone who's interested know all about that, and I feel, Jeasus, it's either the drink, but yes at this moment in Flanagan's lounge I feel fierce sorry for Ernie.

At last he has the drinks organised and is turnin' to deliver them, and I catch his eye, and say howareye and he says, 'Great form . . . Breda,' he'd be the type to remember names, do his best, Evonne ignores him totally as he sets the gin down in front of her and he doesn't deserve that, no one deserves that.

Their daughter Imelda Egan has arrived with Geraldine and her sister Jennifer Cullen who just this morning is back from Australia, accordin' to Eilish, and they're dressed to kill, skimpy tops and glitter and make-up, I can see heads turnin', lads nudgin' lads, as they head down through the main body of the bar.

Eilish says me name, 'Breda, are ye still with us?' 'Jeasus, I am, rarin' to go,' I say. But on the way out, on the way up to Mac's, the ol' stomach is knottin' again, and the head is full; of Billy up at the bar, knockin' them back, noddin' over, but never comin' over, disappearin', and me sittin', nursin' a drink and cursin'. I try and black this out, get rid of it . . .

'Breda, are ye all right for a dance?' That's what he'll say, through the dry ice, like he used t'do, and then he'll bring me home. I look across the road, see us walkin' home together on that bit of the street, past the chipper's and Tommy Taylor's menswear, that will be it, me and Billy, in about two hours' time, he might even take me up on to the canal bank.

Eilish spots that I'm away with the fairies and she grabs me arm as the other two laugh and clip-clop ahead up the town. 'Ye look great,' she says and it feels good again, me and Eilish, arm in arm, headin' up the town and Billy, me husband, will arrive up to meet me, above in Mac's.

Billy   Shoutin' at the bar, over the din comin' from the disco at the far end of Mac's, shoutin' for drink, shoutin' at Feggy and the Eoghan puttin' green fella, 'We're gonna drink some porter tonight ja mouch,' shoutin' at Brefine, 'Ah sure them English wouldn't drink spring,' but we will, in the centre of it all, Mac's, Sunday night, the last lap of the

holy trinity and I take a swalla and we move down towards
the seatin' area, gettin' nearer to where Breda and Eilish
and all them are; and I suppose it's kind of weird to see her
out again – and I turn to the Eoghan fella and say, 'Do ye
see your one over there agin the wall, second from the left,
she's takin' a sup of her drink, there, now, do ye see her?
That's my one, me trouble and strife, what do ye think of
her?' and your man is lookin' over at Breda, really takin' her
in like and he's leanin' back into me now and he says, 'She's
a very attractive woman.' Well, Lord Jeasus, I burst me hole
laughin' and that's no coddin' or jokin' and I says, 'Do ye
think so? Well, Jeasus, maybe ye'd like to take her off me
hands so, huh, a young fella like ye.'

He kinda smiles and says somethin' that I don't catch 'cause
Feggy's roarin' somethin' in me ear, and I can hardly hear
him either the music is that loud. 'Did ye hear' . . . 'Girls
just' . . . 'Billy, did ye hear about' . . . 'wanna have fun' . . .
'Did ye hear' . . . 'Hear fuckin' what?' I roar back and then I
see her on the floor, givin' it the full trip with the Cullen
sisters, Imelda Egan in a little top, and bits of sweat on her
face and I get that rale excited feelin' again . . . Feggy's still
roarin', '. . . about the Big Banana?' 'Wha'?' 'Big Banana.'
'Wha' about him?' I'm listenin' now. 'Therese the mot is up
the pole, and they're all up above in the house, all the
Bananas, celebratin', so he's not comin' out tonight,' and
Brefine is behind us and he roars, 'I hope they'll all be very
happy,' rale smart like, 'cause Therese is the mot that he got
into trouble with the Bananas over, and Feggy roars back,
'Don't get fuckin' smart now, you,' and Brefine laughs and
I'm delighted that there'll be no row, or am I, maybe half of
me is a bit disappointed that I won't witness Brefine Grehan
and the Big Banana squarin' up to each other.

Imelda's still up on the floor, girls just wanna have fun, I'm
on track, take a swalla, very near to Breda now, and I'm so
on track I'm thinkin' that I can afford to sit down with her
for a minute, it'd be odd if I didn't, like, so I do and she's all
smiley, a bit mickey and, Jeasus, she is lookin' well, done up,

like, and she's definitely lost the weight, Eilish says that she's rale happy to see us out together, I ask where Tony is, she says that he had to go to Dublin, I nod, rememberin' a course that Tony has a one on the go in Dublin, a blondie one, and I smile, James Galway, it's a pity he won't be around tonight to see me gettin' off with Imelda Egan. I spot her sittin' back down with the Cullens, lightin' a smoke and Breda lights a smoke and she off them this long time.

Eilish turns away so it's like the two of us, and we haven't been out like this in a good while so I kinda say that she's lookin' well, 'cause she kinda does and she's pleased and she tells me that Eilish and Tony had a great night last night, and that she was pleased for Eilish 'cause the English fella she'd left had been a woeful thick bollocks. I tell her about Eoghan, the puttin' green fella and about the chat I had with Brefine and we seem to be gettin' on fierce well and I go up to get more drink, passin' by Brefine and the Eoghan fella chattin' ninety to the dozen. Feggy remarks that Breda's lookin' well and I can't help bein' a bit chuffed, because when she had the weight none of them ever mentioned her.

When I get back the last slow set is comin' on and Breda wants to dance and I don't 'cause I don't want Imelda to see us out on the floor so I say that I have to go to the jacks and I'll get the last ones in on the way back but I can see that she's browned so I say, and this just comes out, I say that I will come home with her tonight, for definite, and she smiles and gives me a kiss, which is twice in one day, so things are gettin' a bit outta hand.

Breda   Outside Mac's, Therese is tryin' to get Sandra to go in for one and a dance before they head up to the 'I'm pregnant' party. 'Jeasus Christ, Therese,' says Sandra. 'You're the one who's havin' the fuckin' baby, you'll have to go up.' 'Ah Jeez,' says Therese. 'They'll all be so locked up there now they won't give a fuck where I am.' 'No fuckin' way, Therese,' says Sandra and starts to give out to her that the only reason she wants to go into Mac's is that Brefine

Grehan's back in town and she had a thing with him last year which nearly drove Big Banana stone mad. 'And I'm not takin' no shite from Big Banana for lettin' you go in there and not bringin' ye up to the party.' Sandra is gettin' thick now so Therese gives up, they say their goodbyes and head off for the Bananas' house and we can hear Therese sayin', 'I've no fuckin' interest in Brefine Grehan, he's fuckin' mad, are yes jokin' me.'

Me and Eilish laugh as we get inside the door of Mac's and pay our fiver. It's Sunday night but the girl is singin' 'Saturday night and the air is feelin' right, be my baby'. They've changed the place around a bit since we first danced here, in them days it was fairly rough, Jeasus, I remember this band from Dublin that came down one time, doin' covers of Queen songs and the singer thought he was great, the beezneez, until the Mule Mulvin made shite of him. The singer had been over tryin' for Eilish, Eilish was havin' none of him and that's when he tried it on with the Rat, Finnegan's mot, which was a big mistake as the Mule was the Rat's cousin and he proceeded to make mincemeat of the singer.

Anyways, we've found seats, good seats, in at the wall, 'cause it's not that packed yet, there's only a few young ones on the dance floor at the back, so I have a bit of time to settle in before Billy arrives, to start really enjoyin' the night, and I ask Eilish does she remember the whole Mule beatin' up the singer incident and she says that she does. She sings the chorus of 'I want to break free' and says, 'He wanted to break free that night when the Mule got hold of him.'

She heard off Tony that the Mule got an extension to his sentence in Portlaoise 'cause he broke into the mental hospital next door and had a go at some retarded woman and I go, 'Lord Jeasus, Eilish, that's fuckin' desperate, is that the sort a thing talk he was usin' to charm ye last night?' 'No, I'm just tellin' ye what he heard, that's all.'

I can't help askin' her, 'So is it true about Tony?' 'What?'

she says. 'Ye know, what they say about him.' 'What?' 'Ye know, the man with the golden flute,' and I burst out laughin' and Eilish is shakin' her head at me. 'Jeasus, Breda, what are ye like,' and with that she says that if I really want to know . . . The golden flute is a fair sight when it gets goin' but it takes a fierce amount of work to get it there and a lotta encouragement to keep it there. She signals over to Rosey Robinson to get us more drink and then she goes on a bit about Tony, that at the end of the day he's sound, but not averse to ol' yarns to the boys to bolster up the James Galway name.

I take a drink and I think of how much of that ol' shite Billy might believe.

I look across and see him up at the bar standin' with Brefine Grehan and the fella, yeah it was the fella that I'd seen with Ernie Egan in Flanagan's earlier on, and they're halfway through pints and I'm smilin' at Eilish, lettin' on as if I don't give a shite and sure whenever he comes over, he comes over. And Eilish winks at me. 'Good luck' . . . Rosey Robinson arrives with drink for us and how it's murder up at the bar and how Feggy Fennelly was tryin' to chat her up, again: 'Lord Jeasus, remember I snogged him at the Debs.' And I see Billy, closer now, with Feggy shoutin' somethin' in his ear and I'm lookin' at Rosey's cigarettes. Jeasus, I'd love one, I'd love to light one up, get up, go over and ask Billy out on to the floor, slow set, 'I know this much is true'.

Rosey and Eilish laugh at somethin' and Eilish nudges me about to tell me whatever it was they were laughin' at when I look up and there's Billy, and Eilish makes room, and he sits down and I feel like it's that first time he came over to me, there's a nervousness between us, which is great, Eilish says somethin' and he asks where Tony is and she tells him and I grab one of Rosey Robinson's fags, light it up, 'cause I don't give a fuck.

Eilish turns away and Billy looks at me, says nothin' for a few seconds and I'm about to make ol' chat when he says,

'You're lookin' well,' and I smile and he smiles and I blow
out smoke and talk about Eilish and Tony and how Cliff,
the English fella, had been such a bollocks, ye know, fillin'
him in, and he's fillin' me in about the young fella I'd seen
him come in with, about how he was sellin' portable golf
greens around the country, and he's tellin' me the Brefine
Grehan yarns and we're laughin', havin' the crack, like rale
crack and he goes for more drink.

Eilish turns back around and says, 'Jeasus, ye were gettin' on
great,' and she gives me a little hug and I look out on the
floor. 'Love is all around us' . . . the slow set . . . 'just let
your feelings show' . . . and I know now, it's clear to me, I'm
sure, positive, certain that he is comin' home tonight, and
I'm willin' him to get back 'cause I'm goin' to ask him, out,
on to the floor, for definite, just a kiss, one long lovin' kiss on
the floor, in front of everyone. He's back over, droppin' the
drinks on to the table and I stand up, don't think about it,
I'm standin', in front of him, 'Billy, are ye right, for a dance,
like,' and I smile and he kinda looks away, then back. 'Have
to go to the jacks,' and he turns to go, and I sit down, sink
down, but he turns back: 'Sure well . . . we'll have a bit of a
dance later on . . . ye know . . . at home.' I spring up so
quick that the drink on the table nearly goes flyin', restin'
me hand on his shoulder and kissin' him on the cheek, and
he's gone, and I'm floatin' now, giddy, takin' a big sup of
vodka to celebrate. He's comin' home to dance with me, not
here, at home, and I wonder what he's thinkin' now, what's
he feelin', 'cause for the first time in ages I think that we
might be feelin' the same thing.

Billy   I'm in the jacks, the head racin', and Scobie Doyle
and Schooner Donoghue are beside me havin' some eegoty
shorthand row about what year Noel Grady was killed in
the car crash, and I'm gettin' the queer feelin' again, 'cause
I'm thinkin' of Breda, and that maybe I will go home with
her, I think of me two girls, and the days they were born,
and the day we got married, all this shite flyin' around me
head until I think I'm gonna get sick.

Breda   The anthem comes on and I have to steady meself to stand up, 'cause I'm fairly locked, Jeasus, I am, he's back with more drink. Anthems over, sit, must tell him, it'll be all right, I'll talk to him, reassure him about . . . ye know . . . the night ahead, and Eilish says somethin' about him not gettin' too drunk, and I laugh and I do, I do reassure him, and I'm squeezin' his hand, 'It'll be different tonight, 'cause I've made the effort, ye know, and so have you,' and I just want to rest me head on his shoulder 'cause I'm that locked now, and he's releasin' his hand and sayin' that he just wants to go over to talk to the boys for a while and I'm smilin'. 'See ye in a sec,' and I blow him a kiss, in front of everyone, fuck them, husband and wife, Billy and Breda.

Billy   I'm out at the packed bar now, and, as l knew there would, there is a party back in Cullens' tonight, 'cause Feggy roars it over to me, and was I comin'? I say that I don't know, rale thick, like, 'cause, 'cause I don't know what the fuck I'm at, and I have to stick me head under the closin' shutters to roar at Celia Kearney for a drink, and they've only large bottles a Harp left so I get one and a Vera Lynn and supersonic for Breda.

When I get back over, they're playin' the anthem and we're all upstandin' and Breda's singin' the few words that she knows. We sit down and Eilish says somethin' to me like, don't get too drunk now, Billy, and she winks, not tonight, and Breda laughs and takes me hand and the hairs on the back of me neck stand up, I can feel them 'cause I know, she's goin' to say somethin', she's gonna mention somethin', and I'm fuckin' right. I take a big swalla and she's sayin', 'It'll be all right, we'll be all right tonight, I know we will . . . it'll be different, 'cause I've made the effort, ye know . . . and you have too.' She's squeezin' me hand, and I try and see her in the paintin', me and her behind the tree, me as hard as a rock, but I can't, I never can, I wish she hadn't said anythin' 'cause I know now that I can't go home with her . . . can't face it . . .

I have to be James Galway, I have to go to the party, I have

to get off with Imelda Egan, get back on track, so I grab me
bottle and say that I'm goin' over to talk to the boys for a
minute, and she smiles and turns to talk to Eilish. I slip up to
the bar and order a naggin and a few large bottles and out
the front door where Noddy Nolan, the bouncer, is tryin' to
talk to his mot Big Ears except there's a minor scuffle about
to start up with a crowd a drunken young gnocs. So I leave
them to it and head across to the town hall. I sit down on
the stone steps, it's coult, rale henny howlt so I take a swig of
the Powers and wait till I see Brefine, Feggy and the skunk
leavin' Mac's where the scuffle is over and Noddy stands
proudly in the doorway wearin' the face off Big Ears.

I run after them and as we all head down the town to
Geraldine Cullen's house for the session, I get a bit of the
queer feelin', 'cause I remember the way Breda had been
smilin' at me. Then doesn't Brefine have to go and mention
am I not bringin' her down, so I let out a laugh. 'Ye don't
bring apples to an orchard,' and I take another big swig,
'cause it's Sunday night, it's the last last lap of the holy
trinity and Imelda Egan is waitin' for me above at the party.

Breda   The place is beginnin' to clear but me head isn't so
I offer Eilish me vodka, lookin' forward to bein' outside;
Eilish chattin' ninety to the dozen, Feggy Fennelly over
tryin' to talk to Rosey Robinson: 'Are ye comin' up to it?'
'No.' 'Ah come on.' 'I'm goin' home, end of
johnnymafuckingorry' and people pass by, a crowd a young
fellas singin' 'You're my wonderwall'. I mouth the words
along with them, and me eye drifts over to the bar, to the
boys, Brefine Grehan, the Skunk, the golf green fella, the
Mouse Mahar and there's no Billy, no Billy. 'I'm goin' up to
talk to the boys.' No sign of him there, talkin' to no boys,
boys talkin', no Billy, me eyes flick to the jacks door, door
bangs open, but no Billy, only Martina Shanley's younger
brother, white as a sheet, which makes me laugh, 'cause he's
so white, like a ghost, but where is Billy?

Because Tony's arrived, James Galway has arrived, out of
the blue, and Eilish is beamin', he tore down from Dublin to

see her, reckoned she'd still be here, and she is, and they
kiss, in front of everyone, and he greets me and then he says,
'Where's the man?' 'The man,' I say. 'The man . . . is, I
think . . . but don't quote me . . . it's not gospel . . . the man
. . .' 'Jeasus, Breda, you're locked,' says Eilish. '. . . The man
. . . is in the jacks.' 'Oh, right,' says Tony and then he puts
on a mock cockney accent. 'There's a party up in Cullens'
for Jennifer, do you fancy it, love?' 'Oh Jeasus, Tony, don't
put on that voice,' and they laugh like a couple jokes
have . . . like a joke couples have and Eilish turns to me:
'I'm goin' to head up, youse are goin' home, aren't ye?' I'm
noddin' me head. 'I'm just waitin' for himself.'

Tony is sayin' somethin' to Eilish, mutterin', now she's
mutterin' and he gets up and goes and I turn into Eilish's
big eyes starin' into mine, words comin' outta her mouth,
careful kinda words: 'Listen to me, Tony's just goin' to
check around, see where he is.' And no sooner have I taken
this in when Rosey Robinson is sayin' her goodnights to us,
tellin' Feggy Fennelly to leave her alone: 'Lord Jeasus,
Feggy, you're pure mule.' Tony's back from doin' his
rounds and I know by the gimp of him that I'll be walkin'
home on me own. He's mutterin' again 'No sign', but I
hear, I hear perfectly, and that confirms that the evenin', the
night, has turned fuckin' mule on me, pure mule.

I light a fag and I stand up and put on me coat and Eilish is
sayin' somethin' about findin' him. 'Where would he have
gone?' she asks Tony and he's rale embarrassed. 'Well, he's
probably gone up to the Cullen sisters' party.' Eilish is all
action now, stubbin' out her fag, gettin' the coat on,
grabbin' the bags, lighter, drainin' drink. 'We're headin' up
there, straight up, march in, show the fucker up in front of
everyone.'

Tony's gettin' worried, James Galway doesn't want a scene,
but he needn't sweat, because I have no intention of goin'
anywhere near and I'm smokin' me fag and tryin' to be
calm because the whole point of the night was that he
should want to be with me, at home, he should want that,

but he obviously doesn't so leave him to whatever it is he
does want, the drink, whatever . . . leave him . . . leave him
to it.

Billy   So we're up in Castle Avenue, in Geraldine
Cullen's, fairly packed, a few holy pictures around the place,
outta respect for the mother who had to go into the old
folks' home the year before, but other than that it's been
done up, a kinda youngish feelin' off the place and, Jeasus, I
must be one a the oldest here but sure maybe that's a good
sign because that means they must really want me here,
even though I'm that little bit older, for a reason, and I
know the reason, Imelda Egan wants me here, it was like I
dreamed it would be.

I drain a bottle a Harp and say 'Please God ye will' to the
Mouse Mahar who's shitin' on about how the long bar darts
team will win the league next month, and I head over to
where Brefine is, good ol' Bref, settin' it up for me, holdin'
Geraldine and Jennifer but most importantly Imelda at the
kitchen door, so I head straight over, straight in no kissin',
'Do yes know this man,' I say. 'Fuckin' mad man,' and a
chorus goes up, 'Course we do after he goin' off with
Therese and Big Banana out to kill him,' and I'm just about
to launch into the time me and Brefine tried to break into
the school but he's in full flow again, finishin' the Blacksod
in London story, except this time Blacksod hasn't fallen off a
fuckin' buildin' at the end, oh Jeasus no, Brefine's a hero
instead, headbuttin' the bullyin' foreman, which has them
all rale impressed, glued to him and I'm standin' beside
Imelda, rale close, she smells a perfume and drink and a
gush of fag smoke, which hits me face as she explodes with
laughter and gowayouttathatin' at Brefine's story which is
over, so I'm rackin' me brains to say somethin', anythin' to
get the ball back off of him but doesn't he ask Jennifer
Cullen about Australia so she starts on about the mad
weekends over there and Imelda leans in rale close to
Brefine to get Jennifer to tell him, just him, to tell him about
the mad fucker from the Fiji Islands and Jennifer screeches

laughin', 'Well, I'm not jokin' yes now but,' and goes on about the Fiji fella.

I'm beginnin' to feel ralely browned when who comes in the back door only Tony and Eilish. 'How's the boys,' I say, 'cause I'm pleased to see them. 'Hello,' says Tony but Eilish walks past sayin' nothin' and I say, 'What the fucks atin' her,' and Tony looks at me and says that she's fierce thick with me for not goin' home with Breda and I say, 'Sure Jeasus, I was always goin' to be up here' . . . He gives me this look, a quare look, not a look I've seen before, as if to say, why the fuck are ye here, Billy? And I try and ignore this and gee him up by sayin', 'Anyways I thought that you'd be with the blondie one, the Dublin one,' and he looks at me again and starts to go and I, I just grab his arm, you know, friendly, like, 'cause he's my friend, and I'm smilin' at him, but he looks down at my hand on his arm and says, 'Jeasus, Billy, don't believe everythin' I tell ye' . . . I'm kinda shocked and let go of him and he passes on towards Eilish and I'm left standin' on me own, me Harp finished and thinkin', 'Ah Jeasus, Tony will come around, whatever is atin' him, at the end of the night when I'm with Imelda Egan he'll take his cap off to me and he'll whisper, "Good man, James Galway the second."'

Breda   So I head on out, out of Mac's into the air and it seems cold, everythin' seems cold and the other two catch up on me and Eilish wants to see me home and I say that I'm grand, and they eventually go off, Eilish still protestin', Tony calmin' her.

I'm not grand, I'm boilin', ragin', clip-clop, down the fuckin' town, on me own, through the arguments and snogs, the roars and shouts. I pass the the chipper, Carmel Connolly still there behind the counter, big red face on her, strangled with the queues. Clip-clop, walkin' on, but seein' meself in me Communion dress inside reachin' up to put the pennies on that same counter. Carmel Connolly smilin' down at me, shakin' and pourin' the salt and vinegar before she'd ask ye did ye want any. Starin' up at her bruised eye

and wonderin' how she got it. 'LOhhhhhh lieeeeeee, the
fields of Athenry' comes bawlin' at me through the air:
Carmel Connolly's husband. The Leaba Connolly is
batterin' me eardrum. 'So lonely round the fields of
CARMALLL!' he's roarin' as he passes me on the way to
the chipper.

Clip-clop, walk on, further now past Freida's fashions,
where Billy once got me a voucher for, past O'Connor's
where he does buy them the sweets, to the canal bank,
where he used t'bring me, where he brought me that first
night. Up on the bank now, don't want to go home, not yet,
cryin' like . . . like . . . I did that time at the Debs.

It was on in the Greville Arms, Ciarin Keating, not the best-
lookin' of fellas, bein' fierce shy but fierce polite and time
and Smithicks ale passed and he danced with me and talked
about business studies in Athlone and he kissed me, rale
beginners like, the pair of us, but at last I'd been kissed,
heart pounded, flushed, Bacardi-and-Coke excitement,
where was Eilish to tell, not on the floor, not at the tables,
had to tell her, not in the jacks and someone says that she's
gone outside, the car park, the coaches waitin' for us, the
cars, I see her with her fella, in the back, windows not quite
steamed yet, it'd be all right to knock, so I did, on the
window, 'Eilish,' I say, 'Eilish!' And the fella shouts
somethin' out at me which I don't catch, then the door
opened. 'PIGARSE, TELL PIGARSE TO FUCK OFF
OUT OF IT!' That had been the name: PIGARSE.

Billy   Tony's with Eilish, holdin' her hand and Brefine has
Jennifer Cullen on his knee and Imelda's laughin' with some
young one and someone's handed the Skunk a guitar and he
starts singin', they all start singin', and I see a bottle of
Southy in the kitchen and start skullin' it, 'Drove my chevi
to the levi but the levi was dry' and I skull some more 'cause
I have to get back on track, get near to Imelda, I skull some
more, 'cause they're all clappin', singin', and I'm on me
own in the kitchen tryin' to remember the first verse of
'House of the risin' sun' but the head's not the Mae West so

I have to lean agin the wall.

There's this picture behind me, googly-eyed now, but I focus in on it and it's fierce like the picture in our bedroom, with the fields and the men workin' and the big tree and I'm thinkin' that I could sing 'House of the risin' sun' and impress Imelda and I try and see her, her, behind the big tree, but I get the quare feelin' again, and all I can see is Breda, me and her in the picture, I hear Brefine launch into a rebel, and it's gettin' all blurry, and me and Breda are there, behind the tree, and we could be kissin', we could be, can't see now, don't want to, I want to see Imelda and I stand up, right in the doorway, 'Get out, you black and tans,' and I can't believe it, here she is, on the last stretch of the holy trinity, the beautiful Imelda is comin' towards me.

Brenda   Down on me knees up on the canal bank now, starin' at the one boat tied up by a rope wrapped tightly around a bollard. Wonder could I free that rope, jump in, sail away, away to the sultan, quick try and loosen the fuckin' things, come on, someone's comin' along the bank, break a fuckin' nail, footsteps gettin' closer, can't shift the rope, the footsteps stop beside me now, can smell smoke and there's a voice, not a voice I know, 'Do ye want a hand?' 'Yeah, yeah, I do,' I say.

'Your boat, is it?' he says, and I'm wipin' the hair, tears, mascara, shite off me face. 'Are you all right?' he says, and I have to laugh, am I all right. I laugh and look up and I'm seein' his face, cigarette in his mouth . . . it's him, it's the golf puttin' green fella, he's offerin' the penknife to me, this total stranger has the penknife held out in his hand waitin' for me to take it and all I can do is laugh, he's sayin stuff about me leavin' the . . . 'Saw you leavin' the disco, on your own,' he's sayin'. I take the penknife in me hand and he says, the stranger says, 'I was talkin' to your husband . . . Met him earlier in the bar, I saw him with ye in the disco and then him leavin' on his own,' I hear the stranger sayin'. And I think of Billy up at that party skullin', devourin', murderin' drink and I think of me two girls hopin' they're all right at home and hopin' so much for them.

'Leave it,' he says, so we do. I'm standin' up, movin' over,
sittin' down, settlin' down, sinkin' down into a bench behind
us and he's offerin' me a cigarette so he mustn't think that
I'm too stone mad. I'm soberin' up a bit now and thinkin'
that maybe he's the mad one, helpin' a woman to steal a
boat at the terminus of the Grand Canal and not knowin;
why.

Billy   So I step into her and start to chat, James Galway,
and she laughs, which is great, on track, I take her arm
'cause I've so much to tell her, but she slips her arm away.
'Go into the session now, Billy.' She slips away, moves on,
away from me, headin' through the kitchen, past the
paintin', to the back toilet. I follow after her, the toilet door
closin' as I get to it. Lean me head agin it . . . try the handle
but it's locked. I so want to show her the paintin', I so want
her to know about us in the paintin', so I do, I tell her about
the two of us, behind the tree, me as hard as a rock, how
she's kissin' me, all over me . . . how all the men in the fields
workin' are lookin' over at us, because they'll all know now.
That I'm havin' Imelda Egan behind the big tree and
they're not. 'Do ye hear me . . . Imelda, can ye hear me,'
I'm sayin' and I knock on the door, then I hear the lock. She
has heard me, the lock is opening, she's invitin' me in. I
push the door and there she is, laughin', sayin' that I'm
stone mad. I step into her and say that I am . . . mad about
her. That she's the most beautiful thing that I've ever seen
and I take hold of her arm again just to try and get her into
the kitchen for to show her the paintin'. I kinda pull at her,
me other arm goes around her waist. The two of us agin the
big tree, at last, it's how I knew it would be . . . Imelda . . .
and me as hard as a rock, I must be, surely to Jeasus I must
be. 'Billy,' she's sayin'. 'Billy' . . . She tries to pull away,
roarin' now for me to let go of her. We stumble, we fall, in
agin the jacks bowl. There's a clatter, blood comin' from me
head, the singin' has stopped 'cause the men from the field
come runnin' over, crowdin' into the doorway of the jacks. I

look up, Eilish standin' over me, with Tony, Feggy, Brefine,
the Skunk and all the others. For a second there's not a
move or a word. Until some cunt lands a kick into me, Jeez
Christ, Tony jumps to pull him back, Imelda frees her arm
and backs off. Then I hear: 'You're a fuckin' disgrace,'
Eilish standin' there, boilin'. I try to get up clingin' to the
jacks bowl and Eilish is roarin' at me now, 'Big hard man,
well, we all know that there's nothin' ever hard about
you . . . ever.' I start laughin', at the whole thing, 'cause the
boys are lookin' at me, but none of them will laugh with me,
none of them will look at me except Tony who helps me up.
I lash out at him. 'I'm all fuckin' right.' Eilish tellin' me to
get out and go home to Breda and I stumble past her, Tony,
Feggy, the Skunk, Brefine, the Cullen sisters, Imelda, the
whole lotta them, past them all and out the front door, me
eyes squintin' aginst the bright, me head spinnin', ribs
achin' from the kick, balance goin', fightin' for to keep
straight, but fall into the gate, nothin' ever hard about me. I
can see them all standin' around the front door, and I'm
about to roar at them that I'm all right and they can fuck off
back inside, but I don't. 'Cause there's nothin' ever hard
about me.

I get up slowly, concentratin' everythin' on standing, have to
walk, one foot in front of the other. Faster now. Gettin'
away from them now, gettin' down the town. Jack Moran is
deliverin' the milk but I can't even look at him because
they'll all know now, in every pub in the town, Kavanagh's,
Mac's, the Corner, Bob's bar, Flanagan's, they'll all know
that I'm not James Galway and that I never was.

Breda   I kinda feel that I should be goin' but he's talkin'
again, why is he talkin' to me, he's bein' nosy now I think.
'Did you and Billy have a row?' 'Fuck off, who are you
anyways to be askin' me anythin'.' 'Me name's Eoghan,' he
says. 'I sell . . .' 'I know,' I says. 'Portable golf puttin' greens,
ye travel round the country with them, somethin' about
your uncle Gilbert and the *Late Late* and Gay Byrne.' He's
noddin' and laughin' whilst takin' out a naggin of whiskey,

openin' the cap, takin' a slug, offerin' me some, which I
accept, heat in me throat now, lovally burnin' as he's talkin',
and it feels like he really wants me to be listenin'.

He's younger than me and he's got dark hair and he's sayin'
that he takes in a lot, watchin' things, comes from spendin'
so much time in different places on his own. I ask what has
him in this salesman crack and he tells me about his uncle
Gilbert who invented the greens. How he'd needed the
work, needed the wander and how his father had
disappeared the year before, for no reason, just upped and
left and how he half hoped that he might run into him,
hidin' out in some town that he'd drive into, some pub he'd
walk into and there'd be his dad sittin' at the bar and how
he'd watch him for a while, study him to see had he
changed, because when somebody you think you know does
something like that, runs away like that, you feel as though
you never knew them at all.

We're both sittin' on the bench now and I take more
whiskey and a cigarette from him and it seems to feel OK
just bein' here. Below us the odd car is speedin' by, or
trundlin' drunkenly home and I swear that I can still hear
the Leaba Connolly screechin' 'The fields of Athenry' in the
distance.

This Eoghan has a moustache and kinda sallowish skin . . .
as far as I can make out and I'm rememberin' a question he
had asked a while ago and now I feel like answerin' it, so I
do, I tell him that no, meself and Billy hadn't been rowin',
that was the fuckin' thing about it, we were ready to make
up until he went off and I'm tellin' him where he went off to
and I'm tellin' him about us, I'm tellin' this total stranger
about me marriage, and the more I'm goin' on the better
I'm feelin'.

He says, 'Billy asked me what I thought of you, ye know.'
'Wha'?' I say. 'In the disco, he asked me . . . about you.'
'About me,' I say, whiskey hittin' me a bit, and this golf
puttin' green totin' total stranger man is sayin', 'I told him

that I thought you were very attractive.' I'm grinnin', and closin' me eyes and listenin' to words, in between the tiny sounds of the water, words like, 'When I saw him leavin' I wanted to run after him and ask him why was he leavin' for a party when he could have gone home with you.'

There's the odd shouts from the street down below, voices I recognise, some that I don't, and someone's singin', a girl, a love ballad, one of the ones ye'd hear a lot, and for this time a night it's odd 'cause she isn't screechin' it, it's kinda sweet . . . and I open me eyes now and I'm laughin' 'cause if I could only tell this fella . . . what is his name? . . . Eoghan . . . if only I could tell this fella, this Eoghan, my husband didn't come home with me because he doesn't want me, he doesn't want Pigarse. But I'm sayin' nothin', I've stopped laughin' and he never was, he's been starin' straight into me face. 'Why would he go off to a party when he could go home with you,' he says again and his face is comin' forward, towards me, slowly, this face that I hardly know, and I close my eyes, as this face joins mine and we're kissin' now, really kissin' now, whiskey tongues, hands graspin', because he wants Pigarse, no , he doesn't want Pigarse because I hear 'Breda', my name. 'Breda', he's sayin' it, 'Breda', he's chosen me, out of all the women in the harem.

We're in the tent and all the guards have left, just me and the sultan and I climb on to him, astride him now, I can feel him, grab hold of the bench because Pigarse is gone, it's just the sultan and me, Breda, ah yes, me and him and Billy is behind us in the tent, tied up in the tent, forced to watch us, and I'm laughin' because he can do his thing and me, I can do my thing. I grab hold of the sultan's hair and it's over now, beautifully over, heavy with breath, both of us, and we kiss.

We're just huddled on the bench now, sayin' nothin', sure what needs to be said but I want somethin' else, before I go home and I know what it is. 'I have to go home soon but if you could just hold me, just here a while,' and he smiles. 'Is that all right, I hope that's all right,' and he nods so we will, we'll stay, just here, just like this . . .

We're there for I don't know how long except the breeze is beginning to feel colder. The first light is comin' up but I still have me eyes closed because I'm pretendin' I'm being loved, really loved. I can pretend that much, but now I'd better get up, so I do. He goes to say somethin' so I lean in towards him and shut him up with a kiss, and then I go. Walkin' back down the canal bank towards home, where I'll pour meself a vodka because I've never felt quite like this before, and I laugh at this, at least for this mornin' I can laugh. So I do. I laugh all the way up the town.

Billy   I'm home. I can feel tears as I open the front door. In the hall now, headin' for the stairs, and I think I see somethin' through the glass of the livin'-room door, or a someone. Looks like Breda sittin', couldn't be, at this hour, no, she'd be upstairs now, asleep. Outside our door, pass by it. Open door to the girls' room, lie down on their floor, can't get up. I'll sleep in here with them, that's what I'll do, with my girls. There's a stirrin', a voice, a little voice in the dark, 'Daddy, Daddy, what are ye doin',' and I shush them and say, 'It's all right, lads, I'm sleepin' in here with ye tonight, just here, on yer floor, is that all right, I hope that's all right with ye.'